Woah! What's the Weather?

Contents

Woah! What's the Weather?

Calling all aliens!

Are you planning a holiday to planet Earth?

Finn and Zeek are here to help.

'Woah! What's the Weather?'
Published by MAVERICK ARTS PUBLISHING LTD

Studio 3A, City Business Centre, 6 Brighton Road,
Horsham, West Sussex, RH13 5BB, +44 (0)1403 256941
© Maverick Arts Publishing Limited May 2019

A CIP catalogue record for this book is available at the British Library.

ISBN 978-1-84886-466-5

www.maverickbooks.co.uk

Credits:
Finn & Zeek illustrations by Jake McDonald, Bright Illustration Agency
Cover: Jake McDonald/Bright, Secheltgirl/Shutterstock
Inside: Shutterstock: Johan Swanepoel (4 & 26), Secheltgirl (6), Iakov Kalinin (6),
ND700 (7),   Echunder (7), Suwin (8), Dmitri Ma (9), Kurkul (9), Repina Valeriya (10),
Suiraton (10 & 11), Kotenko Oleksandr (11 & 12), Creative Travel Projects (12), Vadym
Zaitsev (13), By Mejnak (14), Rovenko Photo (15), Popicon (16,17 & 27), Jhaz
Photography (18), Justin Hobson (20), Evgeny Pylayev (21), Marc Bruxelle (21), Jason
Patrick Ross (22), TasfotoNL (23), Opalev Vyacheslav (24), K.Sorokin (24), Sergei Drozd
(25), SeraphP (25)

This book is rated as: Turquoise Band (Guided Reading)

INCOMING MESSAGE

Dear Finn and Zeek,

I want to visit Earth, but I'm worried about the weather! There are so many different types, I don't know where to start!

Please can you show me some examples and help me prepare?

From,
Dill
(Planet Drull)

The Weather Types

Planet Earth has lots of different types of weather...

Sunny is the best!

...sunny

...windy

...rainy

I like the rain.

...snowy

There are scientists called **meteorologists**.

Let's go and find out more!

Meteorologists have lots of different ways of finding out about the weather!

They use computers to study the weather. They find out about the temperature and rainfall in different places.

Temperature

Temperature is how hot or cold it is.

One way to read the temperature is with **thermometers**. When it is hot, the level in the thermometer is high.

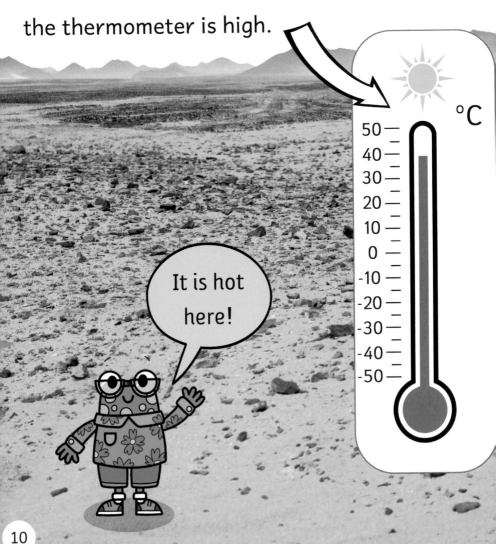

°C

50
40
30
20
10
0
-10
-20
-30
-40
-50

It is hot here!

When it is cold, the level is low.

Rainfall

On cloudy days, rain often falls from the sky.

When it is cold, the rain can turn to snow.

Rain gauge

Meteorologists use a rain gauge to measure how much rain has fallen.

Windy Weather

On windy days, the clouds move fast.

It can go from sunny to rainy very quickly!

This is a weather vane.

It shows which way the wind is blowing.

This weather vane shows the wind is blowing south.

When the wind blows, the arrow turns

to face the way the wind is blowing.

Weather Forecast

A weather forecast tells us what the weather will be in the future. This is based on the information that the meterologists collect.

Symbols are used to show the weather.

 Sunny

 Cloudy

 Rain

 Snow

 Fog

 Wind

 Thunderstorm

 Sleet

17

Bad Weather

A forecast can help people to be prepared for bad weather. **Storms** are one example of bad weather. Most storms don't cause much damage - but some are very dangerous!

Some storms have **thunder** and **lightning**.

Lightning can cause a lot of damage!

Tornados are whirling winds that create a funnel shape.

I am glad humans have ways to forecast bad weather!

Hurricanes are strong storms that can damage houses and blow cars off roads.

Sometimes a rain storm causes a bad flood!

21

Natural Forecast

You do not need computers to study the weather. You can look at the shape of the clouds. Clouds that are dark and low could mean rain.

Clouds that are high and white mean good weather.

There are other wonderful ways of reading the weather...

Birds sing more when the weather is good. Seagulls come inland when the weather is bad at sea.

A red sky at night can mean good weather. A red sky in the morning can mean bad weather is coming.

Some humans believe that bad weather is coming when cows lie down!

MESSAGE SENT

Dear Dill,

There are many different types of weather on Planet Earth. Meteorologists study it all the time!

If you watch the weather forecast, you can find out what the weather will be like before it happens. Then you can avoid the bad weather or put on the right clothes!

From,
Finn and Zeek x

1. What are the scientists called that study the weather?

a) Weather pros

b) Meteorologists

c) Forecasters

2. What can you use to measure rainfall

a) A rain gauge

b) A wind vane

c) A thermometer

3. Does this thermometer show that it is hot or cold?

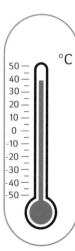

4. What does this symbol mean?

a) Sunny

b) Cloudy

c) Foggy

5. What is the name of a storm with very strong winds?

a) A hurricane

b) A mist

c) A red sky

6. Why are weather forecasts important?

a) So you know what to eat

b) It can warn people of bad weather

c) So you can learn something new

Turn over for answers

Index/Glossary

Fog pg 17
Fog is like a cloud. It is very low and makes it hard to see.

Flood pg 21
A flood is an overflow of water.

Hurricane pg 21
A storm with very strong winds.

Lightning pg 19
This is electricity that flashes in the sky in a storm.

Meterologists (me-te-or-ol-o-gi-sts) pg 8-9, 13, 16
Scientists that read the weather.

Rainfall pg 9, 12-13
How much rain falls in a place.

Rain Gauge pg 13

A way of measuring the amount of rain that has fallen.

Temperature pg 10-11

How hot or cold something is.

Thunder pg 19

A 'boom' noise that you hear during a storm.

Storm pg 18

This is when the rain and wind is very strong.

Weather Forecast pg 16-17, 20-21, 22-23

Finding out the weather before it happens.

Weather vane/ Wind vane pg 15

A way of seeing which way the wind is blowing.

Book Bands for Guided Reading

Pink
Red
Yellow
Blue
Green
Orange
Turquoise
Purple
Gold
White

The Institute of Education book banding system is a scale of colours that reflects the various levels of reading difficulty. The bands are assigned by taking into account the content, the language style, the layout and phonics. Word, phrase and sentence level work is also taken into consideration.

Maverick Early Readers are a bright, attractive range of books covering the pink to white bands. All of these books have been book banded for guided reading to the industry standard and edited by a leading educational consultant.

Fiction

Non-fiction

To view the whole Maverick Readers scheme, visit our website at www.maverickearlyreaders.com

Or scan the QR code above to view our scheme instantly!